Usborne

My First Book

About me

I like dancing!
What do you like?

Usborne Quicklinks

To visit websites with video clips, activities and things to make and do,
go to www.usborne.com/quicklinks and type in the keywords "first book about me".
We recommend that children are supervised while using the internet.

Website researcher: Jacqui Clark

Contents

My First Book

About Me

Felicity Brooks

Illustrated by Mar Ferrero

Edited by Hannah Watson

Designed by Francesca Allen
and Kirsty Tizzard

I am me and you are you

This book is all about me!

I'm Anisha. I live at home with my grandad. Who do you live with?

and me

I'm Joe. I like reading about animals. What do you like doing?

and us

We are Oscar and Oliver. We look the same but we like different things.

and me

My name is Kirsty. I have red hair and freckles. I like skipping.

and me

My family call me Mo. I have black hair and I like maths and dancing.

and you!

and me!

Hello! I'm Valentine and I love to draw. Can you draw a picture of yourself?

Everyone is different

Take a look at all the people around you. No one is just the same as you.

What are your friends like? What are the people in your family like?

Some are GRUMPY, and some are HAPPY.

Some are YOUNG.
Some are OLD.
Some are in between.

Some are short and
W I D E.
Some are tall and thin.

Some wear cool glasses.

What do you look like?

meow

Some have pale skin, some have dark skin, some are in between.
Some have long hair, some have short hair... and some have no hair at all!

5

Me and my day

This is what I do on a school day.

Anisha

After I wake up, I go to the toilet, wash my hands and brush my teeth.

I brush my hair and put on my school clothes. I can dress myself.

After I've eaten my breakfast and had a drink, I feed my fish.

I make sure I have what I need for school and I put on my coat and shoes.

I always walk to school with Grandad. We cross the road at the crossing.

At school we hang up our coats before we go into our classroom.

In our classroom we do drawing, writing, puzzles, reading and numbers.

At playtime we go outside. I like to play with my friends Kirsty and Carla.

This is what Anisha does in the afternoon.

hometime

play in the park

dance lesson

TV time

mealtime

bathtime

story time

bedtime

7

Me and my feelings

Feelings can change during the day. How do you think the children feel in this picture? Choose from the words below. Answers on page 32.

happy   shy   upset   surprised   proud

My plant died!

Valentine

Kirsty

Hi! What's your name?

Anisha

Mo

Anisha

BOO!

Joe

What do you think made Mo feel happy?
What makes you feel happy? When do you feel upset?

Which is which?

Joe has drawn some faces to show different feelings. Are there times when you felt like each of these? What made you feel like that?

angry

sad

worried

excited

scared

happy

Saying sorry

If you do or say something that makes somebody feel sad or bad, you hurt their feelings. You can say "sorry" to make them feel better.

9

Me and my body

Each part of my body has a name. Do you know all these?

head

chest

Kirsty

finger

knee

toe

neck

foot

Try covering the labels and see if you can remember them all.

hair

shoulder

tummy

elbow

leg

bottom

hand

Mo and his friends are pointing to different parts of their faces. Can you point to each one on your face?

eye   ear   nose   cheek

mouth   lip   eyebrow   chin

How do you think these children feel in each picture? Answers on page 32.

a)   b)   c)   d)

Me and my clothes

Look at all the clothes below and help Valentine choose which to wear on...

I can get dressed by myself. Can you?

1 a sunny day

2 a rainy day

3 a snowy day

skirt

sunhat

gloves

sweater

raincoat

boots

trousers

hat

tights

t-shirt

trainers

socks

scarf

sandals

coat

shorts

The friends are each dressed
for a different activity. Can you
match the labels to the pictures?
Answers on page 32.

I feel
excited!

a)

b)

c)

d)

e)

f)

swimming   dancing   football   bedtime   painting   a party

Me and my food

Your body needs some different kinds of food each day to stay healthy.

You need bread, rice, potatoes or pasta to give you energy.

You need plenty of vegetables and fruit.

Eggs, meat, fish, beans, nuts and seeds help you grow.

You need cheese, milk and yogurt for healthy bones and teeth.

Water or milk is best to drink.

You don't need many of these sweet foods as they are bad for your teeth and body.

What I like to eat

These children are feeling hungry. They are telling you what their favourite meal is.

noodles and prawns

chicken and salad

stir-fry and rice

spaghetti and tomato sauce

fish fingers and peas

Can you draw a picture of the meal you like best?

My family and friends

Mo has made a book about his family and friends, and the special people who help him in his life.

My best friend is called Joe. He makes me laugh all the time.

Hannah looks after us when my mum and step-dad are working.

My cousin Ben is very tall and he plays the guitar.

My step-dad is a firefighter but he always burns the toast!

This is a drawing of my cat. She is called Fluff.

Our dog is called Max.

Our neighbours, Doug and Greg, are very nice.

My mum wears funny skirts.

Bella, my baby sister, eats mushy food.

My gran has a pet snake. She calls him Gorgeous George.

My teacher is called Miss Sanchez. She has spiky hair and likes to wear big boots.

If you made your own book about the special people in your life, who would you put in it? How do they help you?

My little brother loves his pirate hat. He wears it all the time.

What I can do

Your body can do all kinds of amazing things.

climb

wave

drink

sit

cry

talk

b-b-bird!

stand

walk

play

jump

count

read

Which of these can you do?

run

KEEP OFF THE GRASS

My senses

Your five senses help you find out about the world around you.

With your eyes you can...

SEE.

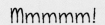

With your nose you can...

SMELL.

With your skin you can...

TOUCH.

With your ears you can...

HEAR.

Look around you.
What can you see?
Can you smell anything?
What sounds can you hear?

With your mouth you can...

TASTE.

19

What am I good at?

People like to do different things and some people can do things better than others.
Do you know what you are good at?

Oscar likes baking cakes and decorating them.

Anisha writes exciting adventure stories.

Valentine is very good at drawing and painting.

Oliver can do all kinds of tricks on his skateboard.

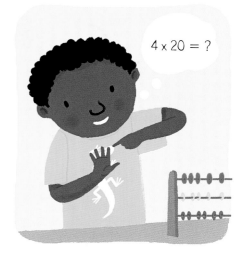

Mo is the best at maths. He likes singing, too.

Joe takes great photos of plants and animals.

Here are some other things the friends like to do.
Which are things you like? Which would you like to try?

eating ice cream

riding a bike

running fast

taking care of pets

dancing

playing computer games

reading

baking a cake

singing

collecting things

judo

flying a kite

climbing a tree

swimming

splashing in puddles

skipping

playing football

bouncing

doing cartwheels

We like looking at the stars.

Growing and changing

When you were a baby, you could only do a few things, but as you grow up, your body grows and you learn to do more and more.

When Joe was a tiny baby, he could sleep, poo, wee, cry and drink milk.

Then he learned to sit and eat food. He grew teeth and started to feed himself.

Next he learned how to crawl and then to stand up. Soon he could walk.

DUCK!

He began to say a few words and then lots. (Now he knows thousands!)

He learned to use the potty and then he started to use the toilet.

Soon he could run, jump, dance, climb and say some numbers and colours.

At school he is learning to read and write and to do maths.

When he's older, he'll be able to go to school all by himself.

Joe Age 1
Joe Age 2
Joe Age 3

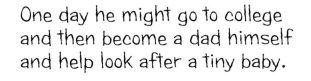

One day he might go to college and then become a dad himself and help look after a tiny baby.

What do I need?

The friends are talking about things they want and things they need. Do you know which page is which?

Clothes and shoes to keep me warm and dry

Friends to play with

Someone to help me learn the things I need to know

Things to keep my brain busy and help me learn stuff

Somewhere to wash and use the toilet

Clean water, and food to keep my body healthy

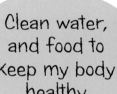

A doctor to help me if I am ill

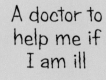

Someone to look after me

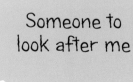

Exercise and fresh air

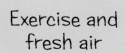

A safe, warm, dry place to live and sleep

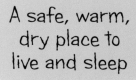

Computer games all day

10 dogs and 15 cats, a hamster and some lambs

My own helicopter that goes wherever I want

As many sweets as we want

22 sparkly party dresses

1,000 presents every birthday

Chocolate cake every day

A ginormous television as big as a house

52 pairs of new shoes

A t-shirt for each day of the year

All about me

This is a page of a book Kirsty made all about herself. What would you put in a book about you?

I love my sister, Sophie.

I like skipping.

Name: Kirsty Trellis

Things I don't like

peas

Pets: Bob (dog)

Bob has a waggy tail.

slugs

smelly shoes

My school: Ockton Primary School

FROGS ARE THE BEST!

My friends: Anisha, Mo, Joe.

My hobbies: painting and drawing

About me quiz

Can you answer these questions? Look back through the book to help you, if you like. The answers are on page 32.

1. These pictures are muddled up. Can you put them in order to show what Anisha does in her day?

a) bedtime   b) breakfast time   c) schooltime

2. Can you match each child to a feeling?

a) happy

b) shy

c) upset

Kirsty   Mo   Anisha

Body game

Mo, Kirsty and Oscar are dancing.
Do you know the names for these parts of their bodies?

finger   knee   head   foot   elbow   chest   hand   toe   hair

Growing up

These pictures show what Joe could do at different ages.
Can you match the right label to each picture?

1.

2.

3.

a) Joe learning to read and write at school.

b) Joe learning to walk all by himself.

c) Baby Joe tucked up in bed and fast asleep.

Food quiz

Can you put these different foods into the right group?

cheese

apple

potatoes

doughnut

meat

1)

2)

3)

4)

5)

Wants and needs

Do you know which of these are wants,
and which are needs?

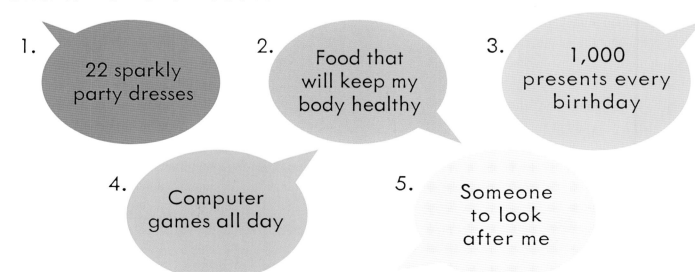

1. 22 sparkly party dresses

2. Food that will keep my body healthy

3. 1,000 presents every birthday

4. Computer games all day

5. Someone to look after me

Index

Answers

p.8 Me and my feelings Valentine — proud; Kirsty — upset;
Mo — happy; Anisha — shy; Joe — surprised.
p.11 Me and my body a) hot; b) cold; c) ill, or sick; d) sleepy, or tired.
p.13 Me and my clothes a) swimming; b) painting; c) a party;
d) dancing; e) football; f) bedtime.
p.27 About me quiz 1. b) breakfast time; c) schooltime; a) bedtime.
2. a) Mo; b) Anisha; c) Kirsty.
p.28 Body game a) finger; b) elbow; c) foot; d) hand; e) head;
f) toe; g) hair; h) chest; i) knee.
p.28 Growing up 1. b); 2. c); 3. a).
p.29 Food quiz 1) potatoes; 2) apple; 3) cheese;
4) doughnut; 5) meat.
p.29 Wants and needs 1. want, 2. need, 3. want, 4. want, 5. need.